AVAILABLE NOW
from Lerner Publishing Services!

The *On the Hardwood* series:

Atlanta Hawks
Boston Celtics
Brooklyn Nets
Chicago Bulls
Cleveland Cavaliers
Dallas Mavericks
Denver Nuggets
Detroit Pistons
Golden State Warriors
Houston Rockets
Indiana Pacers
Los Angeles Clippers

Los Angeles Lakers
Memphis Grizzlies
Miami Heat
Minnesota Timberwolves
New York Knicks
Oklahoma City Thunder
Phoenix Suns
Philadelphia 76ers
Portland Trail Blazers
San Antonio Spurs
Utah Jazz
Washington Wizards

Hoop City   *Long Shot*

Basketball fans: *don't miss these hoops books from MVP's wing-man, Scobre Educational.*

These titles, and many others, are available at www.scobre.com.

 Lerner ™

To Order • www.lernerbooks.com • 800-328-4929 • fax 800-332-1132

ON THE HARDWOOD

PETE BIRLE

On the Hardwood: Cleveland Cavaliers

MVP Books
2255 Calle Clara
La Jolla, CA 92037

MVP Books is an imprint of Scobre Educational, a division of Book Buddy Digital Media, Inc.,
42982 Osgood Road, Fremont, CA 94539

MVP Books publications may be purchased for
educational, business, or sales promotional use.

Cover and layout design by Jana Ramsay
Copyedited by Susan Sylvia
Photos by Getty Images

ISBN: 978-1-61570-902-1 (Library Binding)
ISBN: 978-1-61570-901-4 (Soft Cover)

TABLE OF CONTENTS

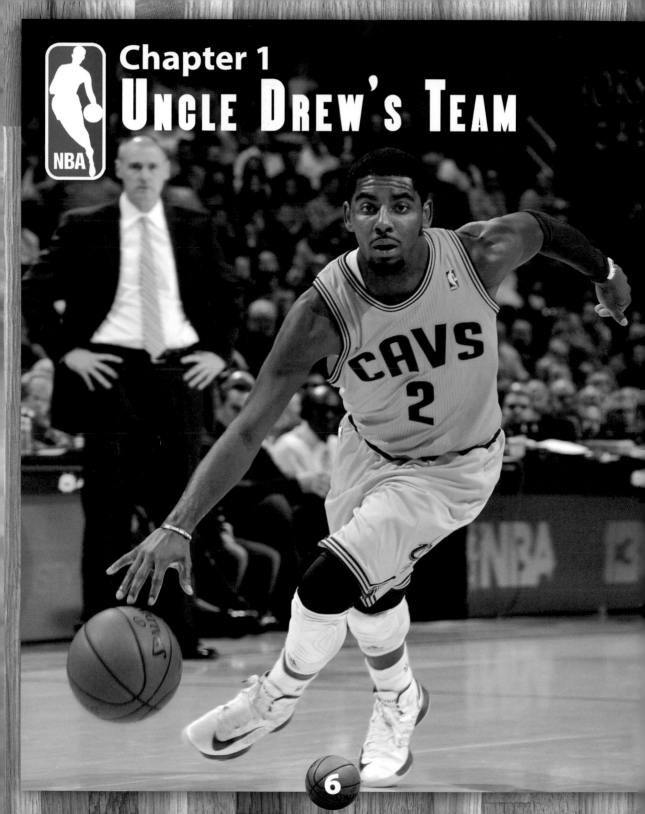

Chapter 1
UNCLE DREW'S TEAM

You may have seen the Pepsi MAX commercials on TV or on YouTube. In them, an old man with a white beard takes a bunch of young basketball players to school, first on a playground in Bloomfield, New Jersey, then on a court in Crenshaw, in South Central L.A.

Named "Uncle Drew," the old man makes the youngsters look foolish as he drives to the hoop, dunks and drains long-range jump shots. Reunited with some of his old-school buddies, he teaches his opponents how the game should be played.

Only, it's not really an old man. It's Kyrie Irving of the Cleveland Cavaliers, the 2012 Rookie of the Year, an

All-Star in 2013 and one of the most talented, all-around gifted players to come into the league in some time. Wearing makeup, glasses, a white beard, and a white head of hair,

One of the most dynamic and talented players in the NBA, Kyrie Irving—the face of the Cavs—has star power.

Irving's alter ego shows how much Kyrie loves the game—and just how special he is. He is at home in front of the camera. To the NBA and fans alike, he has that unique quality: star power. Simply stated, Irving can do it all, both on and off the court.

Perhaps the best ball handler in the NBA, the point guard is nearly unstoppable when taking it to the hoop. Whether it's a spin move, a crossover, or a dribble between his legs or behind his back, he is as skilled as anyone who has ever played the game. Picked #1 overall in the 2011 NBA Draft after playing just one year at Duke University, Irving is a bona fide superstar. Already in his short time in the NBA, he has put his stamp not only on the league, but the Cavs' future. He is the team's undisputed leader—the core of

Irving, perhaps the best ball handler in the league, was the 2012 NBA Rookie of the Year.

an electrifying young squad that fans across northeastern Ohio are counting on to bring the Cavaliers to the Promised Land.

Irving was supposed to be the four-year linchpin as Duke Coach Mike Krzyzewski continued his reign as college basketball's winningest coach. But the heralded phenom, who was raised in New Jersey and starred for perennial high school powerhouse, St. Patrick's in Elizabeth, played in only 11 games for Coach K. After starting the first eight games of his freshman year (averaging 17.4 points and 5.1 assists per game), Irving went down with

Although injured for much of his freshman season, Irving helped take the Blue Devils to the NCAA Tournament's Sweet 16.

a toe injury. He ended up missing 26 games, returning in the NCAA tournament to average 17.7 points in the Blue Devils' three matchups. He poured in 28 against Arizona in the Sweet 16 before declaring for

Campus Tour
Irving played just one year at Duke University before declaring for the NBA Draft—and going #1.

Rising Star

Irving's inaugural campaign was more than worthy of the NBA Rookie of the Year award. He also was MVP of the Rising Stars Challenge.

the NBA draft and going #1.

As far as where Irving's considerable talents can take the Cavs, he will have some help along the way.

Forward Tristan Thompson was picked three spots after Irving in the 2011 Draft. Thompson was a talented and versatile power forward who starred in his single season at the University of Texas. Though he didn't receive the accolades of Irving, Thompson would go on to lead all rookies in offensive rebounding and was voted to the All-Rookie Second Team.

Irving's award-winning rookie year was a special one. He was the MVP of the BBVA Rising Stars Challenge at All-Star Weekend, going eight-for-eight from three-point range. He led his team with 34 points. Thompson led his with 20, hitting 10 of the 11 shots he attempted. In his first NBA season, Irving averaged 18.5 points and 5.4 assists per

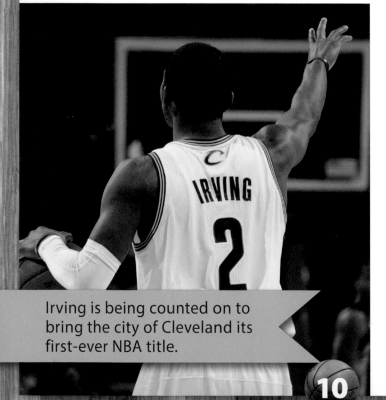

Irving is being counted on to bring the city of Cleveland its first-ever NBA title.

game—joining legends like Oscar Robertson, Magic Johnson, and Allen Iverson as the only #1 picks to post those numbers as a rookie.

Thanks to the Cavs' rookie class of 2011, the future looks bright for the Cavaliers.

But the duo isn't the only reason folks are smiling in Cleveland. The Wine and Gold have tabbed four more first-rounders over the past two drafts. Dion Waiters and Tyler Zeller were both All-Rookie Team performers—as were Irving and Thompson. And this past year, the Cavs won the lottery—for the third time—in the 2013 Draft. The team picked explosive freshman Anthony Bennett of the University of Nevada

Las Vegas with the top overall pick and Russian sharp-shooter, Sergey Karasev, with the 19th overall pick. The prospect of acquiring even more young talent has Clevelanders buzzing with excitement.

Cleveland fans are emphatically devoted to their teams, even though the clubs haven't always given them reason to be. It has been 49 years

Anthony Bennett was the #1 overall pick in the 2013 NBA Draft.

Moondog, the Cavaliers' mascot, gets the crowd pumped up during a 2013 game.

their jokes. Hollywood even made fun of Major League Baseball's Indians (who haven't won a World Series since 1948) in the "Major League" film franchise.

But no city in America embraces the underdog role like Cleveland. Fans in this diverse metropolis are some of the most loyal, dedicated, and passionate in all of sports.

For instance, the Browns are known across the country for their rabid fans. The "Dawg Pound," located in the east end of the bleachers at First Energy Stadium, is home to the team's most vocal supporters, who often wear dog masks and chant, "Woof! Woof!"

From June 12, 1995, to April 4, 2001, the Indians sold out 455

since a Cleveland franchise has won a professional sports championship. (The most recent: The Browns' National Football League title in 1964.) This often makes Cleveland a professional sports' punching bag. Late night talk show hosts regularly insert Cleveland as the punch line in

Underdogs Unite!

Despite not having won a championship in nearly half a century, the fans in Cleveland are some of the most passionate in all of sports.

regular-season home games at Jacobs Field (which has since been renamed Progressive Field), a Major League Baseball record that was later eclipsed by the Boston Red Sox.

And the Cavs have their faithful following as well. The team's streak of 102 consecutive sellouts at Quicken Loans Arena—affectionately called "the Q"—only recently ended in 2011.

Simply put, Cleveland fans love their teams unconditionally—no matter the close calls, near misses, and heartbreaking losses. They've suffered mightily, but they're loyal. They're resilient. They're tough. And they're optimistic that the title which has eluded them all these years is within grasp.

"Uncle Drew" and the Cavs just might give it to them.

Cleveland fans are among the most loyal and passionate in all of sports. And they love their Cavs.

Chapter 2
THE MIRACLE OF RICHFIELD

They were some of the greatest names in the history of the NBA: Bingo, Campy, and Foots. Joined by Austin and Nate, their claim to fame was a 1970's funk-influenced style of basketball that featured creativity and individual expression. Their game was cool, like smooth jazz.

They called what they did "Instant Offense," and it came together like a hit song in 1975-76, when the Cavs—in just their fifth year of existence—made the playoffs for the first time in franchise history. Their masterpiece is known in Cleveland and around the NBA as "The Miracle of Richfield."

The Richfield Coliseum was home to the Cavs for 20 years until it was knocked down in 1994. The spot where the Coliseum stood is now an empty field, designated by the Audubon Society as an "Important Bird Area," one of only 10,000 in the world. At the northwest corner of Route 303 and Interstate 271, the building, while

The Cavs' "Miracle of Richfield" team captured the franchise's first Central Division title.

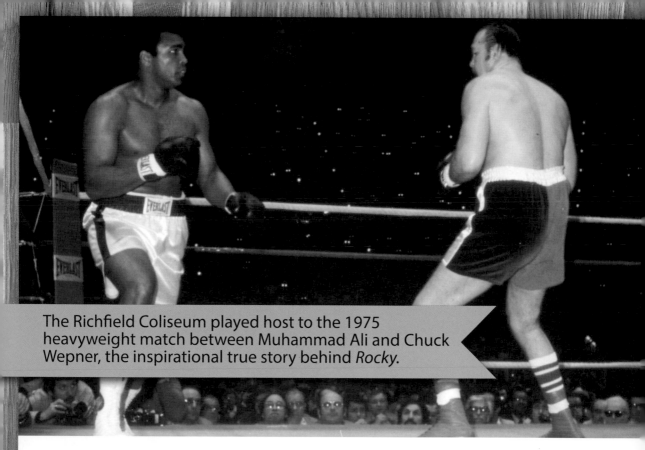

The Richfield Coliseum played host to the 1975 heavyweight match between Muhammad Ali and Chuck Wepner, the inspirational true story behind *Rocky*.

within an hour's drive of more than five million people, was basically in the middle of nowhere. But it held over 200 events annually—from rock concerts to pro wrestling to indoor soccer to rodeos to arena football to the circus—and sold out nearly all of them. The 1975 boxing match at the Coliseum between Muhammad Ali and Chuck Wepner was Sylvester Stallone's inspiration for the 1976 film, *Rocky*.

But more than anything else, it was home to the Cavaliers. And when the Cavs were there in 1975-

Cleveland Rocks

In its heyday, a packed Richfield Coliseum played host to some great events, not the least of which were the Cavs' home games.

76, the place was rocking. The noise during games was so deafening that opposing teams had to come up with hand signals to call plays. Some fans seated close to the floor wore earplugs, and players on the bench plugged their ears with their fingers.

The roar often rattled the pots and pans hanging in the kitchen at Swingo's, the arena restaurant.

Bingo Smith had both a memorable name and afro. He was a key member of the 1975-76 Cavs.

"A madhouse," said Nate Thurmond of the Coliseum. "That's what it was, a madhouse."

The Cavs won 12 straight home games from January 17 to March 13, 1976. And they finished the year 49-33. But they didn't win the Eastern Conference. What they did do, however, was win their first-ever playoff series in seven hard-fought games, three of which were decided at the buzzer.

The so-called "Miracle" season actually began somewhat poorly

Guard Dick Snyder was at his best when playing in the half court.

possession basketball. The second unit—Austin Carr, Campy Russell, Foots Walker, and Thurmond—injected the playground-inspired "Instant Offense" that added a dose of cool to the confidence. The team was well-rounded, and played fundamental basketball—with flair.

"We didn't have any overbearing personalities. That's just the kind of people that we were," said Russell. "It was a real good marriage of 14 guys and a coach. We all came from winning situations, and we all wanted to help each other improve."

for the Cavs, as they won only six of their first 17 games.

But this team was special, and the Cavs quickly found their mojo. The starters—guards Jim Cleamons and Dick Snyder, center Jim Chones, and forwards Jim Brewer and Bingo Smith—specialized in half-court

Under the tutelage of NBA Coach of the Year, Bill Fitch, the Cavaliers created magic on a nightly basis, capturing the imagination of the fans and entering the playoffs with a whole region cheering for them.

"There has never been more excitement and electricity for the Cavaliers down the stretch and into the playoffs than during the 'Miracle' year," said Joe Tait, the Cavs' Hall-of-Fame broadcaster. "The fans rallied around the team, and the team used the fans' energy to propel themselves to the playoffs."

Thurmond, the Akron native and future Hall-of-Famer, was already nearing 14,000 points when he arrived via a trade with Chicago. At 34 years old, he became the Cavs' glue. As the elder statesman on the team, he provided locker room leadership and enabled Fitch's nine-man rotation to gel. Thurmond would go on to be

Bill Fitch won Coach of the Year in 1975-76, using a nine-man rotation that was equal parts fundamentals and flash.

Do You Believe in Miracles?
The 1975-76 Cavaliers captured the hearts of fans with a magical season, referred to ever since as "The Miracle of Richfield."

named one of the 50 Greatest Players in NBA History.

The Coliseum was packed with 21,564 Cleveland fans on April 29, 1976. It was Game 7 of the first round of the playoffs, and the Cavs were facing the Washington Bullets, a team that boasted a host of NBA legends. With future Hall-of-Famers Elvin Hayes and Wes Unseld, who would both be named among the 50 Greatest Players, as well as Phil Chenier and Dave Bing, the Bullets were heavy favorites to beat the upstart Cavaliers. A victory would return Washington to the Finals, where they had lost to Golden State the year before. But it was not to be.

Washington's Chenier tied the game at 85-85 with 24 seconds left. With nine seconds to go, Cleamons inbounded to Snyder, who

Nate Thurmond, here grabbing a rebound against the Bullets, was the elder statesman and leader of the team.

raced past Bullets center Unseld to hit a five-foot runner high off the glass with four ticks on the clock. Chenier fired a desperation shot from the corner, but time expired and the "Miracle" was complete.

Cleveland went on to lose to the Boston Celtics in six games, with Chones on the bench. He broke his foot in practice two days before the series began. The Celtics eventually went on to win it all, beating Phoenix in the Finals.

But the Cavs gave Cleveland sports fans a memory they'll never forget.

"It was beyond fun," said

Campy Russell goes up strong against Dave Cowens of the Celtics in a 1976 playoff game at the Boston Garden.

former Cavs owner Nick Mileti. "It was a miracle."

"Instant Offense"

Even though they lost to the Celtics in the Eastern Conference Finals, the 1975-76 Cavaliers gave fans a memory they'll never forget.

Chapter 3
SHOT DOWN

The Cavs returned to mediocrity again for several years, until they secured the #1 pick in the 1986 NBA Draft. They chose seven-foot center, Brad Daugherty, of North Carolina and, with that decision, a new era began in Cleveland.

With future Hall of Fame coach Lenny Wilkens steering the ship from the sideline, Daugherty led a group of Cavaliers into Cleveland fans' hearts—and into the record books.

A tenacious rebounder with a soft touch, Daugherty was a five-time All-Star and force to be reckoned with. The same year he arrived, the Cavaliers also drafted Ohio native, Ron Harper, with the eighth pick and obtained the rights to Mark Price in a trade with the Dallas Mavericks. Harper, Price, and Daugherty, along with fellow rookie, John "Hot Rod" Williams, immediately began to pay dividends for Cleveland. Daugherty, Williams, and Harper were all

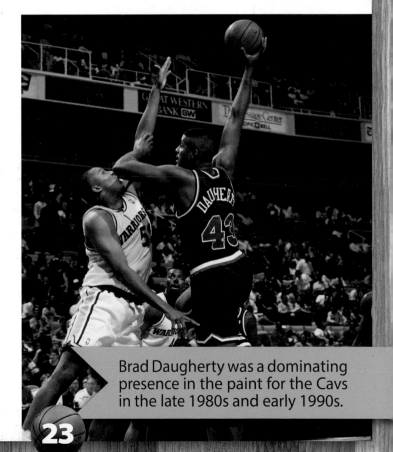

Brad Daugherty was a dominating presence in the paint for the Cavs in the late 1980s and early 1990s.

Danny Ferry was both an inside and outside threat for the Cavs.

Team All-NBA following the 1992-93 season. He made a team-record 100 straight free throws at home from April 5, 1992 to February 5, 1993 and retired as the best free-throw shooter in NBA history.

From 1986 to 1993, the Cavaliers—who also added Larry Nance, Danny Ferry, Terrell Brandon, and Craig Ehlo—challenged the best the NBA had to offer year in and year out. Their team-first philosophy didn't prize individual statistics. Plus, the Cavs boasted a whole lot of talent—and the will to win.

"At the time when we were playing so well, I don't think we paid that much attention to statistics,"

named to the 1986-87 NBA All-Rookie team.

Arguably the franchise's greatest guard, Price was an excellent shooter who became the first Cavalier to be named First

said Price. "We just concentrated on winning games, competing, and doing as well as we could."

"What made those teams special besides their superior ability was they were a team that came to compete every night," added Wilkens. "They wanted to show their fans and the league what they could do on the basketball court."

The Cavs reached the playoffs five of seven seasons under Wilkens, including the Eastern Conference Finals in 1992. They won 50 or more games in three seasons and won a franchise-best 22 consecutive home

games from December 15, 1988 to March 2, 1989. Their 148-80 triumph over the Miami Heat on Dec. 17, 1991, is still the record for the largest margin of victory in an NBA game.

Mark Price retired as the best free-throw shooter in NBA history. Under Coach Lenny Wilkens' guidance, he led the Cavs to five playoff appearances.

Power forward Larry Nance won the first-ever NBA Slam-Dunk Contest, a feat that earned him the nickname "The Ayatollah of Slamola."

Unfortunately, the Cavs were in the Central Division with two excellent teams, the Chicago Bulls and Detroit Pistons. Starting in 1987-88, either the Bulls (with Michael Jordan) or the Pistons (with Isiah Thomas) went to the NBA Finals six years in a row. Cleveland often lost to one or the other in the playoffs.

"We were always winning and playing well, so well that no one could stop us when we were healthy," said power forward Nance. Nance was an excellent mid-range shooter and inside threat who won the NBA's first-ever Slam Dunk Contest, earning him the nickname "The Ayatollah of Slamola."

Perhaps the most heart-breaking loss was to Chicago in Game 5 of the first-round of the 1989 playoffs. The reason is known, in Chicago and especially in Cleveland, as "The Shot."

Replayed on television sets across the country hundreds of times to the agony of Cleveland fans, it was only one basket, yet it played a key role in the fortunes of both NBA franchises.

One of MJ's defining moments, "The Shot" came at the expense of the Cavs, who were highly regarded as one of the NBA's best young teams, ready to challenge for the NBA title.

In their way stood the Bulls,

also a young team. Led by Jordan, Chicago was just beginning to mesh into the unit that would dominate the NBA in the 1990s. The Bulls had finished fifth in the division with a 47-35 record, but they had beaten

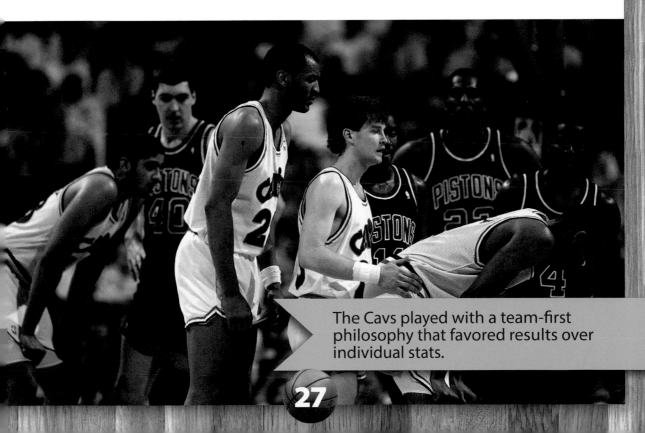

The Cavs played with a team-first philosophy that favored results over individual stats.

Craig Ehlo was a solid offensive player who always drew the Cavs' toughest defensive assignment.

have closed it out at home. But Cleveland rallied for a 108-105 overtime win in Game 4 to set up the deciding game in Cleveland.

It came down to the closing seconds. As he would do time and again over the course of his career, Jordan had the ball with the game on the line. Starting from the right side, Jordan dribbled toward the key and rose up for a jumper from inside the circle. Ehlo, one of the Cavs' top defenders, leaped out to block the shot, but Jordan seemed to hang in the air until Ehlo was out of his way. Then, he let it

the Cavs in a five-game playoff series the year before.

Chicago stole the home-court advantage in the best-of-five series by winning the opener and could

Michael Jordan leaps and pumps his fist in the air after scoring the winning basket over Ehlo, in what became known simply as "The Shot."

fly. As the ball dropped through the net, the lasting image was that of Jordan pumping his fist as Ehlo—and the rest of the city of Cleveland—slumped to the ground, their heads hung in disbelief.

Two years later, the Bulls captured the first of their franchise's six NBA titles. Cleveland, meanwhile, had yet to reach the NBA Finals—until they won the lottery and drafted perhaps the greatest basketball player in a generation.

Lottery Pick

Things were looking up when the Cavs won the lottery and drafted perhaps the greatest basketball player since Jordan.

Chapter 4
KING JAMES' COURT

On May 22, 2003, the Cavaliers were awarded the #1 pick in the NBA draft, the result of having finished 17-65 in 2002-03—tied for the worst record in the league. But such dark days were a distant memory once Russ Granik, former deputy commissioner of the NBA, opened the envelope that contained the Cavs' logo.

Cleveland fans were hoping the lottery ball would fall their way and, when it did, there was no doubt: LeBron James, the high-school prodigy from nearby Akron, would be wearing a Cavalier uniform.

Coming off a spectacular career at St. Vincent's-St. Mary's High School, one in

Prodigy

By picking high school standout LeBron James with the #1 pick in the 2003 NBA Draft, the Cavaliers' fortunes turned around overnight.

which he led the Fighting Irish to several state championships, James was already projected to be an NBA superstar.

LeBron James was considered the best high school player in the nation while just a junior at St. Vincent's-St. Mary's High.

Because so many alumni, fans, and scouts (both college and pro) wanted to see James play, St. Vincent's-St. Mary's regularly played their home games at the University of Akron's 5,492-seat capacity Rhodes Arena. Time Warner Cable even offered St. Vincent's-St. Mary's games to its subscribers on a pay-per-view basis. By the time he was a junior, James was already considered the best high school basketball player in America, as well as the first-ever underclass prep player on the cover of *Sports Illustrated*. By the time he made the transition from St. Vincent's-St. Mary's to the NBA, he was labeled by former *SLAM! Magazine* editor-in-chief, Ryan Jones, as "the most hyped basketball player ever."

LeBron proved to be more than hype. The 6'8", 250-pound man-child was certainly physically ready for the pounding he would get on a nightly basis. But he also brought a mature skill set to the NBA. A strong rebounder and tenacious defender, James was already an excellent passer,

LeBron was not only a physical specimen when he joined the NBA, he was a mature player with all-star skills.

thanks to his superior vision on the court. Perhaps the best part of his game, though, was his drive to the hoop. James attacked the basket like no one else, displaying a superhuman-like combination of speed, power, and leaping ability.

Cleveland fans got a glimpse of that talent in James' first game as a Cavalier. After just nine minutes into the game against the Sacramento Kings, LeBron had already scored 10 points. Then, with less than two minutes remaining in the first quarter, he stole the ball from the Kings' Mike Bibby and fed teammate Carlos Boozer for a dunk. Moments later, LeBron stole it again, ran the length of the court and threw down

This tomahawk jam that James threw down in his first game in the NBA showed everyone he was special indeed.

a monster tomahawk jam. Photos of that shot would appear on posters and blogs almost overnight and is still one of James' signature moments.

Less than a minute later, LeBron made another steal and, despite having a clear path to the basket,

"King James" would hand out turkeys every Thanksgiving to Ohio families in need.

six rebounds, and four steals. Although the Cavs lost 106-92, there was no doubt that the reign of King James had begun.

And his impact stretched far beyond his exploits on the court. Every Thanksgiving, James and his teammates would hand out turkeys and bags of groceries to families in need. He donated refurbished basketball courts to a local community center. And he regularly read to kids as part of the NBA's "Read to Achieve" program. More recently, he purchased uniforms for all the athletic teams at his high school alma mater and donated $1 million to renovate the gymnasium, which will be called LeBron James Arena.

held the ball for a second before dishing it off to Ricky Davis, who slammed it home.

"Sometimes the coaches tell me to be selfish, but my game won't let me be selfish," said James.

In the end, he set an NBA record for most points scored by a prep-to-pro player in his debut, finishing with 25 points, as well as nine assists,

The team's success, with James

leading the way, immediately benefitted the city's economy, too—and not just in television revenue and jersey sales. According to Positively Cleveland, a tourism group, each Cavs game meant $3.7 million for the city. Multiplied by 41 home games, that's more than $150 million.

What could not be measured, however, was the pride, hope, and inspiration the Cavaliers gave "C-Town," one of several Midwestern manufacturing-based cities trying to re-create its image in the wake of high unemployment.

James was appropriately named NBA Rookie of the Year, the first Cavalier to win

the award, and joined Robertson and Jordan as the only players in NBA history (at that time) to average at least 20 points, five rebounds, and five assists per game in their rookie campaign.

East Fourth Street is the place to be to watch a Cavs game—and celebrate another victory.

As Good as Advertised

James was named Rookie of the Year, scoring more than 20 points per game and helping the Cavs improve 18 games from the year before.

With James leading the way, the Cavaliers began assembling veteran talent around their young superstar. Cleveland improved 18 games during James' sophomore season but failed to reach the postseason.

OHIO HISTORICAL MARKER

BIRTHPLACE OF ROCK 'N' ROLL

When radio station WJW disc jockey Alan Freed (1921-1965) used the term "rock and roll" to describe the uptempo black rhythm and blues records he played beginning in 1951. he named a new genre of popular music that appealed to audiences on both sides of 1950s American racial boundaries – and dominated American culture for the rest of the 20th century. The popularity of Freed's nightly "Moon Dog House Rock and Roll Party" radio show encouraged him to organize the Moon...

THE ROCK AND ROLL COMMISSION
THE OHIO HISTO...

Even though Cleveland is the birthplace of rock 'n' roll, it was LeBron James who gave "C-Town" a boost.

But LeBron continued to sharpen his game the following season and the Cavs hired defensive-minded head coach, Mike Brown. Together with an improved roster, Cleveland returned to the postseason in 2005-06, the franchise's first playoff appearance since 1998.

In his playoff debut, James recorded a triple-double with 32 points, 11 rebounds, and 11 assists in a victory over the Washington Wizards. The Cavs would go on to beat the Wizards in six games— with guard Damon Jones hitting the series-clinching shot in overtime, to give the Cavaliers their first playoff series win in 13 years. James averaged 35.7 points per game against the Wizards. But Cleveland was ousted by the Detroit Pistons in the next round.

The following year, the Cavs finished with 50 wins for the second consecutive season and entered the playoffs as the Eastern Conference's second seed. Two playoff rounds later, they squared off against Detroit in the Eastern Conference Finals, in a rematch of the previous year. With the series tied two games apiece, King James made his presence felt like never before in Game 5.

With a boisterous Detroit crowd cheering for their hometown team, the Pistons could only muster a one-point lead at the half. Midway into the third quarter, Detroit jumped ahead 65-58, but the Cavs responded to tie it up at 70 on a last-second three-pointer by rookie Daniel Gibson.

LeBron started the fourth quarter on the bench, getting a much-needed breather. When he returned to the court, he was unstoppable. James quickly scored seven points to get the Cavs within one. Then, with 30 seconds remaining in the game, James dunked to put the Cavs up, 89-88. Pistons' guard, Chauncey Billups, responded with a three-pointer to put Detroit up by two, 91-89. But LeBron sliced his way through the lane again, to throw down yet another thunderous jam just before the buzzer to tie it up

Worthy of a King

LeBron's performance against Detroit in Game 5 of the 2007 Eastern Conference Finals was the stuff of legend: James scored 29 of his team's final 30 points, in a double overtime Cavalier win.

LeBron James gives his trademark chest pump after another Cavalier victory.

the ball with his body. With his legs wide, he banked one in off the glass to give the Cavs the 109-107 victory. Amazingly, James had scored 29 of his team's last 30 points.

"We threw everything we had at him," said Billups. "We just couldn't stop him."

But it wasn't James who would eventually shoot the Cavaliers into their first Finals appearance in franchise history. That honor went to Gibson, who eclipsed his heroics in Game 5 by hitting all five three-pointers he attempted and scoring 19 of his game-high 31 points in the fourth quarter of the deciding Game 6.

Five days later, the San Antonio Spurs did what the Pistons couldn't. They found a way to stop the

and send the game into overtime.

Every time the Pistons scored, LeBron answered. In the first overtime period, Detroit put in nine points; so did James. The teams headed to a second OT. With Cleveland down 107-104, James hit a fadeaway three-pointer to tie the score. With 11 seconds to go, LeBron got the ball at midcourt and headed for the hoop. He leaped, protecting

Cavaliers and, in doing so, beat Cleveland in the first game of the NBA Finals. The Spurs then proceeded to sweep the Cavaliers for the title, dashing the hopes of Cleveland fans who expected that the team's first-ever trip to the Finals would end with a championship.

The Cavs failed to return to the Finals, despite James' consecutive MVP awards in 2007-08 (the first by a Cavalier) and 2008-09, and the team winning a combined 127 games in those two seasons— the best mark in the NBA over that span. Yet Cleveland fans figured, as long as they had LeBron, the Cavs would

End of an Era
Three years after the Cavs were swept by the Spurs in the NBA Finals, LeBron left Cleveland for Miami.

return…and eventually win the title.

But James, who became an unrestricted free agent on July 1, 2010, decided to take "his talents to South Beach" to play alongside Dwyane Wade and Chris Bosh in Miami.

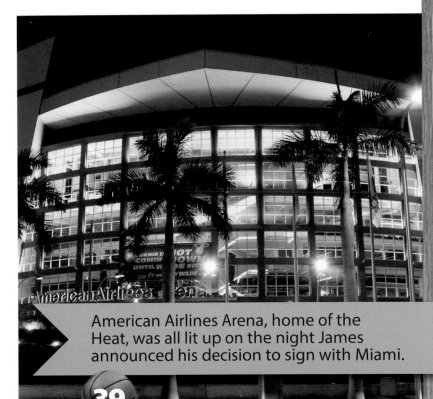

American Airlines Arena, home of the Heat, was all lit up on the night James announced his decision to sign with Miami.

Chapter 5

A New Day for the Wine and Gold

Once LeBron left for Miami, the Cavs were faced with some tough questions: "How can we rebuild? How should we rebuild? And how can we sell our rebuilding process to our fans?"

The Cavalier fan base didn't need much convincing. They have remained as loyal and hopeful as ever. And the franchise, back wearing the original interpretation of the wine and gold, has an NBA title on its mind—and possibly in its sights.

Any such championship will come on the shoulders of Cleveland's intriguing young core of players, led by their All-Star, Irving. Coming into the 2012-13 season, ESPN. com had Irving ranked as the 22nd best basketball player in the NBA. Some felt this ranking was too high, as Irving was just 20 with only one year of NBA experience under his belt.

But Irving has proved the

ESPN.com recently ranked Irving the 12th best player in the league.

A Bright Future

With the talented Irving running the show from the point, the Cavs are looking at good things to come.

doubters wrong. The latest rankings show Irving only improved, jumping up 10 spots to 12th overall. Not the 12th-best point guard in the NBA, but the 12th-best player in the entire league!

Not even the Cavs could have predicted that Irving would be this good, this fast. His upside is limitless and, as he improves, so does the Cavs' playoff chances for years to come.

Having fired Head Coach Byron Scott after their 24-58 season in 2012-13, the Cavs rehired Mike Brown. Brown is the winningest coach in franchise history with a 272-138 mark and a winning percentage of .663—.112 points higher than Cleveland's second-most successful head coach, Lenny Wilkens. The fourth youngest coach in NBA history to win

Cleveland rehired Mike Brown in 2013 with the hope he can recapture the magic of 2007, when he led the Cavs to the NBA Finals

60 games in a season, Brown led the Cavaliers to the 2007 NBA Finals and NBA-best records in both 2008-09 (66-16) and 2009-10 (61-21). Leading the Cavaliers to no worse than the Eastern Conference Semifinals in each of his five seasons, Brown concluded his first go-around in Cleveland with the most playoff victories and highest postseason win percentage in franchise history.

The Cavs are hoping they have another lottery pick superstar in Anthony Bennett of UNLV.

In addition to Irving, Brown will have some talented players to choose from, thanks to two first-round picks—including the overall #1 pick in the draft, courtesy of the Cavs' winning the lottery for the second time in three years.

While Kentucky big man, Nerlens Noel, was projected as the top choice, the Cavs surprised everyone by choosing Bennett, the UNLV frosh who starred for Canada's junior national teams and was the Mountain West Conference

Dion Waiters has emerged as one of the NBA's brightest young stars.

of went, 'Wow!'" said GM Chris Grant. "He does things that you just don't see other people do. So he was always a guy who was highly in our mix throughout the entire season."

Cleveland is also in a favorable position with a strong core of young players, salary cap and roster flexibility, and a bounty of draft picks for seasons to come.

Young players Dion Waiters and Tyler Zeller have already emerged as up-and-coming stars. Guard Waiters was graded as the fourth best overall rookie by NBA.com and was selected to the 2012-13 NBA All-Rookie First Team.

"I'm honored to receive an award like this and it makes me

freshman of the year.

"He was one of those guys, when you walked out of the gym after you saw him play, you kind

Another #1

With team owner Dan Gilbert and his son Nick sporting bow ties, the Cavs won the rights to yet another #1 pick. This time, they took Anthony Bennett of UNLV.

hungry to keep working hard and focus on taking the next steps to improve my game," said Waiters. "I can't wait to get back to work with my teammates and Coach Brown, though, because I'm excited about what our potential can be as a group."

Forward/center Tyler Zeller was named to the All-Rookie Second Team in 2012-13. This was the second consecutive year that the Cavs have had two players named to the All-Rookie teams after Kyrie Irving (first team), and Tristan Thompson (second team), received the honor last year in 2011-12.

All four players represented the Cavaliers at All-Star Weekend in Houston, with Irving winning the Three-Point Shootout on Saturday night. And this past summer, all four represented their country—with Irving, Waiters, and Zeller participating in the U.S. National Team's mini-camp in Las Vegas, and Thompson suiting up for Canada in

Forward Tristan Thompson is a rebounding machine, pounding the glass on both ends of the court.

It's About Time

The Cavs boast a roster of young and talented players who are hoping to bring "C-Town" that long-awaited championship.

the FIBA Americas Tournament.

Waiters averaged 14.7 points, 2.4 rebounds, 3.0 assists, and 1.0 steal in 28.8 minutes per game during the 2012-13 season. Among all rookies, he ranked second in points per game, fourth in assists per game, and fourth in steals per game. Waiters posted 23 points on 11-12 (.917) shooting from the field in the BBVA Rising Stars Challenge at the 2013 NBA All-Star Weekend. He was one of only three rookies to have a 30-point game last season and had 14 games of at least 20 points on the year. Waiters made more field goals and free throws than any other Eastern Conference

Four young Cavalier fans wear their Anderson Varejao wigs prior to a game at the Quicken Loans Arena.

rookie in 2012-13.

As for power forward Thompson, he was inserted into the starting lineup on March 18, 2012, against Atlanta as Brazilian, Anderson Varejao, continued to recover from a fractured wrist. The turning point of his season came in the following game against New Jersey, when he posted a 27-point, 12-rebound performance in a 105-100 road win.

After Varejao was ruled out indefinitely, Thompson started at center for the remainder of the regular season. A rebounding machine, Thompson seemed to grow stronger as the season went on. A career night against the Celtics saw him net 29 points and 17 rebounds while going nine-for-nine from the foul line.

Injuries were a problem for the Cavs during the 2012-13 season, none more devastating than that of Varejao. The 30-year-old center was having a career year and leading the NBA in rebounding at 14.4 per game went he went down. When

Before his season ended in injury, Varejao was leading the NBA in rebounds.

they're on the court together, Varejao and Irving are among the best duos in basketball, forming a nice pick-and-roll combo.

All in all, the Cavaliers have all the pieces to contend now and into the foreseeable future, with a talented roster that might bring Cleveland the title they've been waiting for all these years.

"You take away the positives and negatives and what you need to work on for next season," said Irving. "We'll come back collectively in September and come back a better ball club. That's the main goal."

The fans will be there, as they always have been, supporting their team and their city, waiting to hang that long-overdue championship banner.

As one Clevelander posted on the Internet recently: "I can proudly say: We've got a good thing going on here."

Tyler Zeller is another member of a group of young stars with an NBA title in their sights.